Beau

Amanda Greene

BookLeaf
Publishing

Presentation by *BookLeaf Publishing*

Web: www.bookleafpub.com

E-mail: info@bookleafpub.com

ISBN: 9789357444859

First edition 2023

For past loves that have been lost and to current persons who hold a special spot in my heart. And to the Universe for guiding me on my path.

ACKNOWLEDGEMENT

Here's a Thank You to anyone in my life who's played a leading role or to anyone who's been there through any of the ups and downs, the tears, and the laughter. I am grateful for every single moment. This book wouldn't be possible without you.

PREFACE

The writings in this book were created in times of struggle and over time have come to represent times in life that are like stepping stones. They were moments where I definitely learned a lot about myself, but was also able to gain the knowledge and understanding that goes along with our day to day emotional struggles we face in this life. May you find something familiar within these words and they help you along your path or maybe you'll find just a reminder that you're not alone in what you feel and hopefully, you can take a little insight into our human emotions. May this book leave you with a feeling of being a part of something greater.

LOST & FOUND
(2003)

When all love is lost. When all hope has died.
When your dreams cannot shine.
When all your roads end up closed, and all
you're reaching for is opposed.
Which way to turn - Which guide to take?
Unsure of what will come.
Emptiness deep inside leaves me numb.
When will my skies again turn bright?
When will happiness conquer my night?
Hold onto yourself - Hold on real tight.
Keep your faith and your dark will again turn
light.
Your love can be found, and hope revived.
This is when your dreams can be survived.
Roads will be opened and new paths will be laid.
The Lost was Found -
So real purpose again is made.

DEJA VU

(2007)

Deja Vu — Not just one, but two.

History rotates and the future waits.

Existence unfolds and webs we create.

Deja Vu — Like in my mind, another clue.

Life — Heavens — Soul. All Connected.

Harmony with all that is — Unexpected.

FUTURE – PRESENT – PAST.
WHAT WILL BE WHEN TIME HAS
SUDDENLY BEEN ITS LAST?
DEJA VU – SOMETHING OLD?
OR IS IT SOMETHING NEW?

LOVE/ HATE

(My first love lost (1996)

How can I hate you, yet love you so much?
Maybe it's the feel of your absent touch.
You tried playin' games with me.
Fuck that – I ain't blind. I did see.
All the time I thought you stayed true –
You were out screwing like you always do.
But..you know it's all good – so you better knock on wood.
I won't stoop to your level and be a hater-
But for you I'll no longer cater.
We've tried to compromise – Only to reveal more lies.
In the end, it's best we're not friends. Just know that deep down there will be love my heart sends.

INTO THE DARK
(2019)

A moment in time when your thoughts drift to places forbidden.

What she wanted couldn't be known but they dominated her hunger and she sensed the thought was mutual and not unbidden.

She had to make a move and make it fast.

For her chance would soon be past.

And with barely a blink of an eye she was gone

leaving him a clue, never realizing she'd be back so soon.

She knew her actions were uncalled for.

But she felt them so deeply – she could no longer turn away and ignore.

They snuck away into the dark.

A quiet spot they found – it was the spot that ignited the spark.

That moment in time they fueled a passion so
strong that even if it wasn't right
It surely wasn't wrong.
Time stood still except for the wind amongst
the trees.
Lips to lips and skin to skin as they reached
their height.
They didn't want this moment to end, but the
future had no guarantees.
Imprinted now deeply in their memories was
the passion of their secret paradise.
They each knew without a doubt they'd cross
paths again. They couldn't fight it - now in the
dark- they had their new favorite vice.

BEAUTIFULLY BROKEN

(2021)

She made broken feel beautiful.
And it could only be felt with your soul.
Not broken, but courageous is what she
really felt.
A masterpiece is what she made from all
the pieces of life she was dealt.
Her choices were not always right, but it
was the wrong ones that showed her spirit
how to fight.
She learned that what's meant to be will
flow with ease.
Looking only forward - her mind and her
heart now did appease.

Her purpose in life was not always known.
To accept 'right now' - is what her soul
was shown.
Her past taught her that life shouldn't be
forced -
To be true to herself is what she'd put first.
If being beautifully broken is her destiny
and strength - then it is also her pride she
wears with courage and length.
Her true beauty isn't something that's
been there from the start.
She had to rebuild it and she started with
her heart.
She discovered that such beauty isn't
always kind and loving.
At times, it had to be hard and cunning.
Of all the pieces that had been glued back
together, she knew some shards would be
gone forever.
If moments in life didn't feel like a piece of
her soul - then she didn't want them.
But she'd rise again and be brokenly
whole.

WHIRLWIND

(2017)

My head is like a whirlwind,
spinning out of control.
One more day -
And I think I'll explode.
I want to run, hide, get away.
If I don't, there's a price I'll have to pay.
With a rock behind me and a door in
front....
How do I accept and confront?
To know the way in myself -
there is concern.
I hold the key - which way does it turn?
I hope soon I will learn.

Please someone help me before I lose my mind.
I wish the whirlwinds would simply unwind.
Hopefully tomorrow will clear the way -
So these unwanted rushes in my mind could just run - Run Away

CEASE TO EXIST

You came along and have shaken my
world to its core
Stirring every possible emotion -
yet I still crave more
They say silence is golden
But I hear the silence loud and
clear
Not a word you had intended - No
truth to adhere
Actions speak volumes for how you
really feel
You didn't even care that there was
an unbroken part of me that this
would steal
I stated with clear words to Not
break my heart
Was this just a game to you - one
you played from the start
It didn't take long to notice that
there's something you hide within
And after all the time and effort -
would you ever have let me in?
What hurts me the most is you knew
the love I had for you and the
distance I would go
How I let you fool me has my head
spinning in vertigo.
I hope one day you'll see what
you've missed
Because you and I no longer exist.

SMILE

(2010)

(I have to give credit to my ex-husband for this one. He
wrote the original & I modified it for both "him & her")

Smile - for she really cares about the
person he is.

Laugh - for he will make a fool of himself
for that sweet laughter.

Shine - for she will make him feel like a
star.

Live - for our lives together is really what
matters.

Love - for he is sure to love her ever after.

Cry - for he longs to wipe those tears.

Age - for we look forward to those years.

Speak - for he gives her all of his
attention.

Lead - for she follows his direction.

Follow - for we will find a way to our
perfect love.

Smile - for she is all he thinks of.

PLAYING WITH MY HEART
(2021)

You have to know my walls are now up and my heart
is leary.

For your words of the past have me wary.

How can you say some of the things you do, when in
your heart they aren't true?

Fully aware of things you do and say to me..

Those are things you say when you have the feeling
deep inside of where you want to be.

Why the extra time and extra attention?

For me, that was real - for you it was just an illusion.

I've never felt so used and inconsequential in my
entire life.

It's like publicly you're embarrassed of
me..ouch..deeper goes the knife.
You see....that's usually me in your shoes.
Why didn't I see the hesitation..why didn't I see the
clues.
How often in life do we meet someone where on
every level you have understanding and connection?
Now I question if that was just a game for your own
pleasure and seduction.
There's a side of me you have failed to have opened
your eyes -
With you, the only place I live is under your night
skies.
Maybe the same thing that keeps me in the shadows,
Is the same thing that keeps your heart locked
behind closed dark windows.
Either way, I can't change what transpired.
But I can guard my heart.
Moving forward, I'm still hurt.
Where do I begin again with you - where do we start?

UNTIL WE MEET AGAIN

(2022)

I don't know why, but I feel it in my
soul.
I have to say good-bye for now -
And this you should know
It hurts like hell to walk away
When we cross paths again, I know
it'll feel like we just spoke yesterday.
I write these words with tears in my
eyes.
My heart is going over all the what
if's and all of the why's
What we share is a bond so rare -
No other connection could ever
compare.

Some things cannot ever be put into words
For us this is the unspoken acceptance that our souls use like passwords.
I'm not sure that we were ever meant to be forever, but I know that I'm a better person when we're together.
You have grown on me in ways I never would have guessed
As much as I want you in my life - for now my higher self says I need to walk away and let us rest.
This is not a Good-bye forever - but until our paths cross again.
I'll always cherish what we had and I look forward to the day we meet again.

UNTITLED

(2006)

TRUTH EXISTS
ONLY LIES ARE INVENTED
LIVING – EXISTING
DREAMS INTENDED
ADJUST
JUST NONE
CAN'T STAND IT
LET'S HAVE ALL OR NONE
OBJECTIVE – PERSPECTIVE
LOST – RETROSPECTIVE
CONNECTED AND NEVER ENDED
VISIONS – EQUILIBRATED
SOUL – CREATED

UNCERTAIN FUTURE

Standing here alone
And It feels like there's nowhere to go.
Searching high and searching low.
I feel a warmth from the thought of where I want to be
Actually getting there is what's so hard to see.
I'm uncertain as what is to come or what the future holds
Just going through the motions as each day unfolds.
Hour by hour and day by day.
When will time finally show me the way?
This feeling wakes with me each morning and dances in my
dreams.
All this searching isn't helping, so it seems.
I want to feel the sunshine on my face –
Warming me –
When I'm standing in that absolutely certain space.
Day by day, the uncertainty will subside,
And moment by moment, where I'm going will no longer
hide.

HIS SECRET SIDE
(2023)

His secret side, he hid away for few to
see.

If you happen to be one of the few, it
comes out of nowhere, when you'd least
expect it.

There would be no way to foresee.

Calm and collected is the mask he
presented.

Even with a heart of gold and confidence
in his eyes, he still left me disconnected.

His secret side, I caught with just a
glance

And there I gazed - lost in a trance.

It was there and gone, as quickly as
rolling thunder.

So soft and full of love, yet fierce with
emotion and uncertain wonder.
He shielded his insecurities and built
walls around his heart.
That part of him, he held close.
If used at all it was his last resort.
Still lost in a trance - Left in curiosity
Was this his game or his true modesty?
Unable to peek behind the shield -
His true heart seemed forever sealed.
I will forever wonder if there was a way
to his heart
For me it will remain a mystery - an
always unknown work of art.

MAYBE WHEN

(2023)

Maybe in another hour - another day

Maybe then I won't long to see you stay

Maybe in a different month - another

year

Maybe the fog will vanish and the

uncertainty will become clear

Maybe another time - another space

Maybe the same moon - a different

space

Maybe a spot where time doesn't exist

And we can have all the stars in the sky

to make a wish

Maybe when the breeze is as soft as a whisper

And the angels are singing "please kiss her"

Maybe when the clouds aren't passing us by

And the chaos of life can finally stop and just happily sigh

Maybe when our souls have healed a little more

Maybe when we find a little more peace and can be a little more sure.

Maybe another decade - and more distance between skies

Maybe that's when you and I share a love that's universal and wise.

LIMITED EDITION
(2023)

A lost soul sets out alone

Searching for something they've had all

along.

The search is going to test you and put

you in a tailspin

The key is to find your balance and your

truth within

You'll discover the reality that sets you

free all the while you still keep fighting

that internal war.

Without a clue in the world you'll ask

yourself "Do you know your purpose in

this life and what you are for?

Because once you feel it – It's

something you can't deny or ignore.

When your mind sees the unknown,
trust it and be strong.
Know that your story will go on, even
though the last page is gone.
Your purpose will show your passion
and give you your life's vision
Accept that this journey is meant to
unfold with opposition.
Take the first with the last – and the
last with the first.
This will not be your best nor is it your
worst.
This is your perfect purpose and your
mission
So write your own story – your limited
edition.

BAD DAY

(2022)

(I think it was more like a bad year 🌀)

I think I've seized the wrong fucking day.
Nothing, and I mean nothing, is going my way.
I must've awoken on the wrong side of the bed.
I'm still tired and I feel half dead.
I don't want to adult anymore today.
I think I'll go make a fort and that's where I'll
stay.
I think I've seized the wrong fucking day.
Earlier the sun was shining, then the clouds
rolled in.
Looks like they're here to stay.
I locked my keys in my car and my food order
was subpar.
Please, someone point me to the nearest bar.
I spilled all over my new shirt.
I guess I'll have to go change and miss dessert.
I think I've seized the wrong fucking day.
Everyone please leave me alone
I'll be back tomorrow with a smile on my face.
And "Fuck It" is what I'll say.

SAD SOUNDTRACK
(2023)

I loved you then
And I still love you now
But the past has been broken
To be continuously hurt
I can't allow
I'll forever carry a special spot for you in my heart
I wish you felt the same and that I was more
than just your spare part
I would've given you the world and I think you
know that
But you just weren't ready and your efforts fell
flat
So I guess this is the end - No looking back
I'll just keep on walking
And playing in my ear another sad song added
to my life's soundtrack.

WHAT'S MEANT TO BE

(2023)

What's meant to be will always find its way
Moving life's obstacles
and things not meant to stay
It can move mountains to
help you push through
It can also be tricky and deceive you.
Thinking the false is actually true.
So if you think you've got it all figured out
Think again because nobody has a clue
What's meant to be pushes you along
each path in life
And not once do we really realize that this
energy is larger than life
What's meant to be is always in motion
Leaving in its wake a trail of happiness,
frustration, laughter and emotion
Most pretend and hold their heads high

Not once admitting that they
too are asking why
There are no "what if's" - they just don't exist
All we have to do is accept and admit This life
is grander than any one of us
Surrender and release all doubt- because
what's meant to be will persist
When this power keeps pushing you
to transcend
You can't be too set in your ways -
we all must learn to bend

THIS IS WHY
(2006)

The smile on your face
The gleam in your eye
I love you - This is why
The kiss of your lips
The feel of your touch
This is why I love you so much
Passion in your heart
To your soul I will not lie
I love you - This is why
The smile on my face
The light you shine with each day that goes by
I love you - This is why
The time is near where we'll have to part ways
And I will wish for just one more touch
Just remember-
This is why I love you so much

LIFE'S ROUTE

(2000)

Life brings good- Life brings bad
One minute you're happy - the next
you're sad.
You love - You hate
Comes too soon - Comes too late.
Blessings are sometimes missed in the
blink of an eye,
and all we can do is ask ourselves 'why?'.
This is life's roller coaster ride,
rushing inside you like an ocean's tide.

We still live - We still learn.

Will we shine - Or will we burn?

Just remember, what goes up,

must come down

It'll make you smile,

and It'll make you frown.

Through it all, wear your pride like a

crown.

Wild & Crazy - Cool & Calm.

Visions hazy or the world in your palm.

What does the future hold?

Only our dreams we hope to perfectly

mold.

Good brings bad - Bad brings good.

These fit together to reach a place we all

unknowingly have stood.

Your journey and my journey.

All will forever unwind.

Choose to only follow -

Or total control of your mind.

What about destiny? - What about fate?

These are the unexplored territories we

can so easily hate.

Just know that everything happens for a
reason
so simply like the natural change of
season.
Only to follow the heart and all we feel.
That's what guides us to know all that's
real.
Keep going with time while life moves
on and never ends -
Flowing forever to continue natural
trends.
Like a puzzle with missing pieces hard
to find -
Linking us all together through spirit
and mind.
Know that we are what we choose.
We become by what we do -
and live by what we know.
Making life empty
or making it full.
Whether it's what I choose
or a higher force that's decided for me to
lose -

Most powerful is what you make of it
and the roads you choose.
Cherish little things seeming to be the
odd end out -
Because this is undoubtedly the heart
and soul of life's route.

Printed in the USA
CPSIA information can be obtained
at www.ICGtesting.com
LVHW010931081223
765818LV00076B/2480